W0259741

THE WORK OF DAYS

Sarah Lang

COACH HOUSE BOOKS, TORONTO

first edition

Canada Council for the Arts Conseil des Arts du Canada

Canada

Published with the generous assistance of the Canada Council for the Arts and the Ontario Arts Council. Coach House also acknowledges the support of the Government of Ontario through the Ontario Book Publishing Tax Credit Program and the Government of Canada through the Book Publishing Industry Development Program.

LIBRARY AND ARCHIVES CANADA CATALOGUING IN PUBLICATION

Lang, Sarah, 1980-
The work of days / Sarah Lang.

A poem.

ISBN 978-1-55245-189-2

I. Title.

PS8623.A523W67 2007 C811'.6 C2007-905193-6

For Julie, Noah
and especially Gabriel:

A pulped tree
for the possibility
of art –

With all possible gratitude.
With all possible love.

PART ONE

Hibiscus, hibiscus, hibiscus, rolls
of a hip, an eye remembers like a
great flowering: (this is my big break).

It is 4 a.m. It is early morning. It is summer and so it is already light. And it is warm. You have everything.

A field guide, not given to overstatement, lists broad,
strong wings. Folding blueberries into batter; the dog's nose
is up my skirt. The taste of benzodiazepine and/or paroxetine.

We had chemistry, if not a future. You tell the story. Your hand within hairs' reach. In comparison, I'm largely asexual. I am largely asexual. Eating berries saved from batter. It would have never occurred to me. The feeder near empty. The dew not evaporated. I wish you wouldn't wear that.

What I must look like. A red glass bowl. A spoon. I am not pregnant. You say I would look beautiful pregnant. The low taste of dried apple. The juice of an orange run down my wrist.

If this fails, I will have nothing. I will have left nothing.
Oh, with the way I've been sleeping, I mean.

We broke this body in a pact. For all
your intentions. We made a deal. You and I.
We had a sort of contract involving this body.

That doesn't mean you're off the hook.

the fruit, flower of
the shape
the use of

There were cycles, signs. Now dishes drop,
legs are bruised without rhythm. Tired
does not mean sleepy. This is no summer:
a season is that which passes, which comes.

I wait by the phone; I check and recheck the
line; I weather what never changes. And dreams?
Dreams are no different: work continues, efficient.

chop wood, carry water

I'll not be the woman come wading. Come pant legs cuffed. Come delivering.

Trucks go by. Thunder goes by.

Which is precisely my point. Your hand cool glass. The kids thrown out in the yard. We're out of tomatoes.

Your tucked starch. Think I don't know my own line of youth? Not so fast, mister smarty pants. Slipped into family.

Shake my head. Drag you and that cheap kayak in.

The taste of methamphetamines. I'm clean out of apologies.
Proceed. Your lawn art: steel sculpture, the odd bowling ball
and pin. The postal service threatening you. Shovel. Light
through thinly sliced rhubarb, a pear, bread. Asthenia. Cutlery. A thin
waist. Water over plate. Over ceramic basin.

This that outpouring of colour.
This that body broken.
This that stretched.
This that phosphorescence.
This that even now.
This that lie.
This that smooth floor.
This that crude pleasure.

Your arm around a white, plastic chair.

I read etiquette books so I say 'dream' in place of 'hallucination.' Only one problem per visit. This terrible barrenness and/or ruptured cyst(s). You may be lecturing. And/or nausea. A fascination with Splenda. The cut lines on my back and/or generalized fear with fists numb by morning.

We had a pact, according to your ability that is.

You swore an oath.
You could or could not have known better.
You made judgements.
You were only so able.

You were so happy.
You never changed.

What placed you here. What is reflex, light,
we live in your memories. I squint in your
figurative shadow. Tea you can handle. The light
a great battle. Tell you what, finish something.
The feeder, the chickadees with a great
precision. Oatmeal for itching; onion
for insects. A prayer of determination, as though
there were other kinds. Protect this meagre shell.

I am overmedicated. I feel overmedicated.
I am being overmedicated. I was most definitely
overmedicated. I mean I thought I felt
I could be overmedicated. I thought I was over –

overmedicated, I mean. I thought I felt.

Hadar before Antares. Altair before Acrux. There is art
you can't touch. Can't lean right up into. Look

point by point. You calculate with precision. I accept
your eager trot. I probably sing you. My skin

a stretched hide. Upward from the cheek. Of taste
conjured. If talent fails. What is real, what is hallucinated

emotion. A house, a bicycle, an uneven brick walk. What
is present, proper. The way I've been sleeping.

of tile, marble
of cracked glass
of razor
clean
of Arborite, comfort
of maple, strand
of small, fine
of line prepared

Enough to say mind your beauty. Pallor. Blush.
Doesn't mean you're off scot-free. Start at the apple
and sweep upward toward your hairline.

how swallows fly
how the moth
how caterpillars
how they go

A shell.

A kettle as symbol of calm broken.

Failed the bulb held in hand.

Failed each motion of civility.

I lost concentration.

An empty glass.

Expectation lingers as a loose floorboard.

The weather will not turn.

What I have lost.

What is reflex and what is choice. Smile. The flowers
droop. The vase not the correct height. Take
greater care. But we speak. Light through leaves,
you tell a story. I'll not be the woman come. Once

my interest carried on as a tired child. As ritual
in a dead tongue. The way the light off a leaf,
I laugh, you reach for emphasis. I slice
lemon. The lines of your hand. The sound of water
filling a narrow glass.

In the movement of my arm a line opens.
As an unused window there is no grace. Tell me
if this hurts. The days are occupied. Motion

marks time: a human hand, a branch. I wait
like a lover. Turnips and carrots keep well
buried in sand. What I have endured. A dew

turned last frost, weather. Tell me if this hurts.
What this feels like, if it hurts. When I press. I promised
I wouldn't write. The blood of a cut line. The cool glass.

Glacial. A fine eye line. Railing. One. Come
close. This will change. You say I would look. Left
like this late light I will never be a mother. A blue

wall. A making of space. Containers. A thin shell,
waist rising. Off the hook. Scot-free. The kids
thrown out. Gladiolas. A stone

smoothed over. The art you can touch. Flannel. The warm
handle of a car door. Or, a quarter cup of rice. The calories
in tea. Fireweed. The coast on which an arbutus peels.

The process of not having remembered differs greatly from that of forgetting: there is no record to misplace. Of light or of light

filtered. What is necessity. Today a slow sequence. A pale cheek to pale tile. Today green. White. White. White. Green. In slips, lists. By rote. Today I slept. A movie slips. What is real, what is

hallucinated. The motion of a line opening. What I must look like. Today I took it easy, which doesn't mean there is nothing to be done.

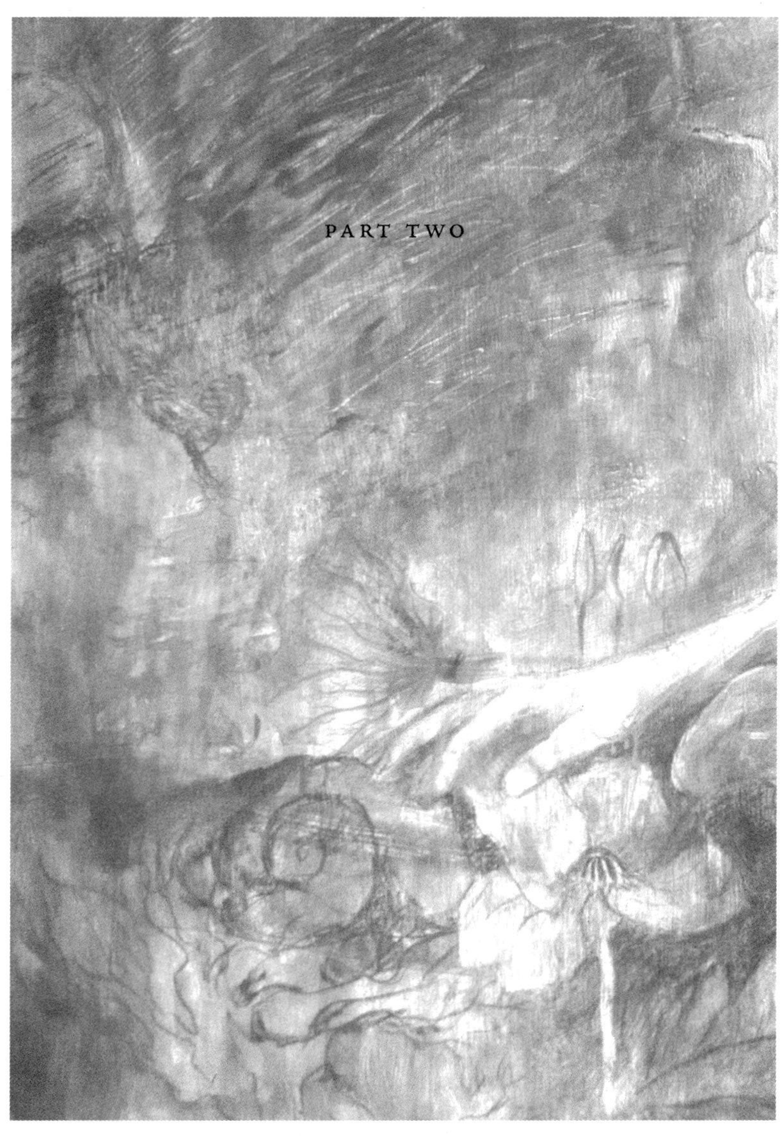

PART TWO

For three inches, I turned the knife in your neck. I watched
with the word *covet*. For forty-five days, I missed your hair.

In a borrowed apartment, I held this contentment. You gagged
as a slit shell. Your eyes opened as the blue wing of a jay, as
yawn. My tongue in your ear listened to your throat

sing. Those weren't scabs you fingered, but you always did sail
clean on through. For your olives and dry cleaning. For your happiness,
I opened as an unused window, without grace and wailing.

Words like sand before your lips;
touch. There are keys, are
ways: I was taught. I was told

so. Help. I see: brick wall, marble
table, black sofa. We do sit,
sand in our teeth. You chew,
swallow crafted. There are no

signs, screams in excess of
touch. This a hand, your
mouth, more than my body.

If this doesn't, if nothing.

To each according to your
ability, according to your means.

We have no curtains. On the twenty-seventh floor,
I roll my knuckles along your jaw. I was once
inelegant. You knew what you taught. A red vase
with modern arrangement. The view. Desipramine,
lithium carbonate. I don't know if I'm polite. I have lost
perspective. The labels are scratched off; your eyes
are closed. I'm sure there are trees. That there is wind.

with frogs made
with female
with the seed of white poppy
with camphor clean and
with clean and
with legs apart
clean, with wheel
goes eye
with waxen
with a stone called
coral, with a house dove
clean
with the hidden part
of a lung

Next to your shin I'm hairless. Take the edge off, blue
as a steel beam. Bear down. Friday: mace and crocus,
carnelian, cooking. My leg opens cold
as a prayer. I'm largely contorted; I am largely
wrong. You've tied my feet. But you never did
hear a word I said. This is not determination.

Hepatica, my lips blue-eyed grass. Sonata.
I used to sleep unaided. Four weeks
and a day. Neisseria, your breath crawls.

This is the harbour where I rig your happiness. One thing
into another: you cover my mouth; I play dead. The sheet breathes
and I do not. For twenty-eight days, I pierce an artery, I wring

your joy. While you're up, I wring your joy. With faint
obligation, I wring your joy. As a rope hangs silent
and without forgiveness, with ease, I wring your joy.

For twenty-eight days get your hands dirty. Near the shore,
tear the flesh from a wild bird. Carve soapstone. Walk thrice
where thieves are hanged. Iron your own shirt.

for feet distorted
for needle
for thrust flesh
for strife, dove bone
for river eel, a sword
for bronze discord
for the third dove
for soapstone diligent
for void flesh is silent
for pure

will flee that place, hold
for

if we hold
if fetuses like unborn
parchment

With each simplification, with a smoothed
curve, with a discarded spike you broke this

body. This my body. Your body is also
finite, yet you claim cure in approximation.

Your error was not significant in that a grace
independent of your alchemy is not,
statistically, that is.

One thing I eat becomes another. The
calories; the spores on the wall weren't our
fault. I commissioned a painting. Eye like a jay
hops, not unlike your thought. Your shawl
of an arm. I don't blame you. The bonsai
were half off. In the heat, you confused plastic
with the fruit of any grunted labour, blood
with the juice of an orange.

if nodules are of the apple-jelly type,
lupus; if lycanthropy, schizophrenia

My back opens on what you demanded. I part
as though this were not difficult. A headlight
circles. We ate dinner after nine. You read

and read fragments aloud, but you never did
hear a word I said. This is the space we agreed
to want. Your hand around my spine; what

I have wrung. The food is now cold. As nerve
from nerve ending, my lips separate. You are certain
I am laughing.

I make soup. I make bread. I hold a red bowl. I study scalded. I hold. I gasp. I sit in front of a cake. I tell a story three times. I offer a dessert fork in exchange for a blind eye.

Your tongue grew like an arc of light
in the curve of a glass has everything.

There were expectations. I was not always
so lazy or so focused on your success.

This brain like a broken arm.

As a neck bears a hand there was a lawn
or children instead of scars. All woods
and balsam, all thure and camphor, all
run down. My word run down. My word
firmer than your sleep. My word
as the weight of grace holds. As the weight
of grace under. As the weight of resignation.

You said I would look; that I was
amazing housewife. I did laundry
much faster than an ordinary person.

will flee that place
and hold, punctured
will flee that gasping

But here, light begins as water rising

to break as a body falls. A chinook
over patched ground. You are

as a ghost, a stray hair blurred
in a photograph already gone. How

to remember
and in what hue.

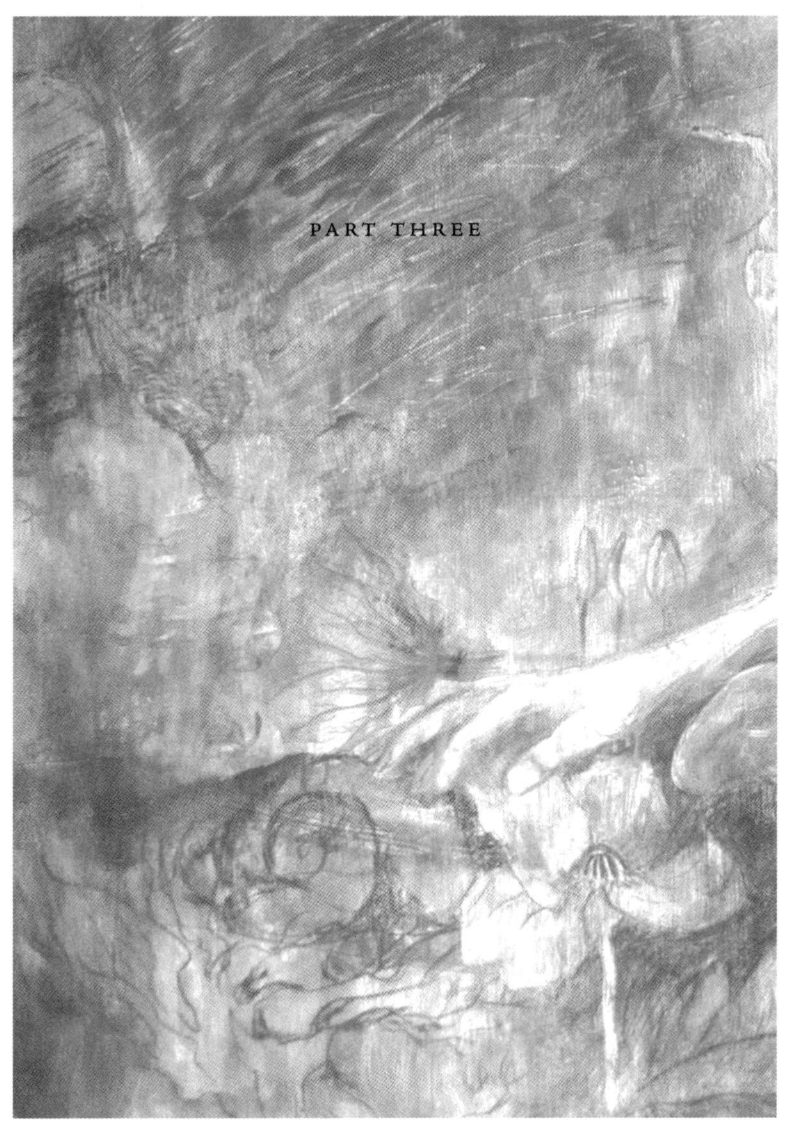

PART THREE

In a city of glass the airport is no different. Lines open like a voice
amplified without guilt. So we have designed possibility; the morning
I call spring; this tree; everything O but through glass, everything

in warm gasps. We ate with eyes that moved as things do: the future
moves, light moves. From clock to watch, hands move. And to

mouths. Trees like a door left open for air: alveoli without treason and
such scent. Good-bye, in our two languages. In our two languages, light
warmed this morning I would have called, without hesitation, spring.

We lit our buildings as your body, through
and against an overwhelming burglary, our gates
closed for the storm. I couldn't hear you

breathing over the TV. What I mean is,
we put forth an effort of normalcy. We did
or did not have dinner. If I remember all

the details, the pear on the counter
curves as your palm. I will never move past
grass blade or bedsheet.

As water fills a glass, I am tired. Of course,
there are limits, light; you thought I was
light come through pear slice, glass; a red

bowl. In the kitchen I collect your shed
scraps. I move without grace, with gum
and glue, I move on hunches, all for you

who call me out. Where did I go? The movement
behind each window. Argon for heat. An opal
for remembrance, for the ability and for risk.

When your skin a callus birch. When we calculate
well. There is no art but skin, no art but
comfort. A warm couch. Clean, there is no art;

your skin is clay shining. I have repainted this wall
three times. When you were carved. When you were
saved. When I knew the taste of your salted neck.

I would like to say you felt like a couch.
I do not mean felt as in touch. In a taxi
your skin shone. When it is hard to go back.

So we have designed
place. A postcard:

a tree, one red bird, a sky
in plain view. Uniformed
in rooms, we turn, lit.

My hand on your shoulder. Comfort,
how home is built. I use the staff

washroom; I am not lost so I must
belong. I am comforted; I

comfort. Monographs like symptoms are readable
on bodies. An old metaphor. Home

is what is readable, known. I knew
your body. I know the chances.

if whether this fell
if pin, gardens
if laugh's forgiving satin
sheen
if neat passes
if neat, bone
if feel and choice to
if of parts
will better
if better a tactile
grouping, if
angled in a way
is a home is a spring
in health

Mountain Ash. I can name the plants. The wasp
around a drink. Your arm tracked and thin. I
squint. The phone does not ring. You are wrong,

all. There is a small dog. I look through a window
at your retreating figure. An empty chest cavity,
an outpouring of colour. Your death is sickness

without nurses. In a pale room, I turn back; I look
through a dull mirror. I held a human heart is somewhat
true. Held, in a room of glass, open for movement.

if line parts
unlike water which
if bedded
stop is never if
scatters a word
contrary, procession
if pond, tree, if a tree
if a smooth tundra
if, to recover lines
your inhalations, gagging

The flight path of swallows, snowfall, is as your wrist
in the red in the lining of a coat. Think of skin as a runway

in dusk. In a room with a shallow closet, clothes hang
on an angle. On a pale, stretched ward, as a body

you were impossible. If I could draw a line around that
time, here as elsewhere, light is as a principal dancer: superior

and surgical. There are names, but a name is a name
is a name. I would like to know like the taste

of rhubarb in pie. But names run together: I will dress
in the dark. I will have left. I will have nothing.

if lily root, bud
if a flat
if narrows and if
round, caw
if caul held
if when a rain
clears sand
if an eyelash, door frame
if a companion lay bare
in roots, meadow
and with purpose

that I have not

so I prayed
so I built

a shrine, a
tower: remember

and if this

forgive that I have not always heard
that I have heard

Ravaged as a starched sheet

is damaged, is part

of the process; is rendered

as light is splayed; so light,

bone is changed, as thread

so sheet, skin is transparent.

Admittedly, there are ends. I no longer wanted. There are ways
to sign season, home; a body is not tender. I knew change; no,

things grow where they will. To what use? You mimed
movement with the skill of one who has moved. A snail

without shell bruises and bruises easily. Our house is thin,
flat flesh. I never could have swallowed all expectations,

or yours. You were the first instance. Where fall
flames, that is flowers, your bones like the trees

are a new season. A chest blooms with demands.
A body is erstwhile in its delicate, radiant finery.

The city has drawn a blank. How big
you are; a tarmac in the cool summer.

You pretend to love them all. *Let*
is a word like a creek in spring.

We are strangers; there are ways
to lie. There are trees, there are

trees, there are trees. The wind
does many things. A Hungarian sign

is not unlike your mouth. I never claimed
gravity, strength. From the left, a cot

has great significance. Like the city
we squeeze in tight for a photograph.

Acknowledgements

Portions of this work have appeared in *Conjunctions, Verse* (online) and *Spire;* for this I thank the editors. For the time and resources to write this work, I thank the Literary Arts department at Brown and the Alberta Foundation for the Arts.

About the Author

Sarah Lang was born on a Saturday in the winter of 1980, in Northwestern Canada. In the spring of 2004, she completed her MFA at Brown University. She began work on her PhD in Chicago in the fall of 2005. Her work, which includes poetry, prose, personal, critical and medical essays, has been published in Canada, Great Britian and the United States. She has translated work from Latin, Ancient Greek, French, Ukrainain, Japanese and Mandarin. This is her first book. She now lives in, and writes of, airports. She intends to orbit the earth before her projected death in 2056.

www.arimneste.com
theworkofdays.com

Typeset in Adobe Jenson
Printed and bound at the Coach House on bpNichol Lane

Edited for the press by Kevin Connolly
Cover art by Hannah Donovan
Cover design by Stan Bevington

Coach House Books
401 Huron Street on bpNichol Lane
Toronto, Ontario M5S 2G5

800 367 6360
416 979 2217

mail@chbooks.com
www.chbooks.com